ONE NATION,

KNEELS
to Pray

31 DAYS OF PRAYER
FOR OUR NATION

ONE NATION,

KNEELS to *Pray*

THE
POPULAR
GROUP

This book was written by Walnut Grove Press for exclusive use by the Popular Publishing Company.

Popular Publishing Company LLC
1700 Broadway
New York, NY 10019

ISBN 1-59027-066-5

The ideas expressed in this book are not, in all cases, exact quotations, as some have been edited for clarity and brevity. In all cases, the author has attempted to maintain the speaker's original intent. In some cases, material for this book was obtained from secondary sources, primarily print media. While every effort was made to ensure the accuracy of these sources, the accuracy cannot be guaranteed. For additions, deletions, corrections or clarifications in future editions of this text, please write Popular Publishing Company LLC.

Certain elements of this text, including quotations, stories, and selected groupings of Bible verses, have appeared, in part or in whole, in publications produced by Walnut Grove Press of Nashville, TN; these excerpts are used with permission.

All scripture quotations, unless otherwise indicated, are taken from the HOLY BIBLE, NEW INTERNATIONAL VERSION ©. NIV ©. Copyright © 1973, 1978, 1984, by International Bible Society. Used by permission of Zondervan Publishing House. All rights reserved.

Scripture taken from the NEW AMERICAN STANDARD BIBLE®, Copyright © 1960, 1962, 1963, 1968, 1971, 1972, 1973, 1975, 1977, 1995 by The Lockman Foundation. Used by permission.

Scripture quotations marked (NKJV) are taken from The Holy Bible, New King James Version, Copyright © 1982 by Thomas Nelson, Inc. Used by permission.

Scripture quotations marked (NLT) are taken from The Holy Bible, New Living Translation, Copyright © 1996. Used by permission of Tyndale House Publishers, Incorporated, Wheaton, Illinois 60189. All rights reserved.

Printed in the United States of America
Page Layout Design by Bart Dawson
Cover Design: Tiffany Berry

1 2 3 4 5 6 7 8 9 10 • 02 03 04 05 06 07 08 09 10

TABLE OF CONTENTS

One Nation Prays...

INTRODUCTION

*W*e live in a world that is far different from the one of our forebears. Yet, we are no different from earlier generations in one profound respect: we still need God.

This generation, like every generation before it, still turns to God for guidance, strength, comfort, and love. Abraham Lincoln spoke for countless believers when he confessed, "I have been driven many times to my knees by the overwhelming conviction that I had nowhere else to go." But today, we face challenges that Abraham Lincoln could never have imagined.

The complexity of today's world requires vision beyond the capability of any single man or woman, no matter how wise. How, then, can we survive? A.W. Tozer directs us to the answer: "Leadership requires vision, and whence will vision come except from hours spent in the presence of God in humble and fervent prayer?" In other words, if we are to survive and prosper in a difficult world, we must turn our thoughts and our prayers to God.

Today, America desperately needs our prayers. The world in which we live is a dangerous place; the time in which we live is a dangerous time; the forces that seek to destroy us are as determined as they are fanatical. All across the globe, brave men and women serve and protect us, but we, too, must do our part to preserve freedoms we hold dear. And so it is that we—as God-fearing and God-trusting Americans—must follow the lead of Abraham Lincoln: we must drop to our knees in prayer.

This text is designed to assist readers in a 31-day prayer vigil for our nation. For a month, readers are asked to consider the thoughts on these pages and then to pray for the needs of our country. God's Word directs our nation to seek Him and to pray; His Word commands us to turn away from evil and to seek His will. When we do, God guides our paths.

America is strong because Americans have been, and continue to be, a praying people. Now more than ever, we, as grateful citizens of this great nation, must exercise our God-given privilege and responsibility: sincere, heartfelt prayer.

1

One Nation Prays FOR AMERICA

If my people who are called by my name, will humble themselves and pray and seek my face and turn from their wicked ways, then will I hear from heaven and will forgive their sin and will heal their land.

2 Chronicles 7:14 NIV

"*One* nation, under God . . . ." These words are so familiar that we may sometimes take them for granted. After all, God has richly blessed America throughout its history, and why should we, as members of this generation, expect that He would not do the same for us? But, to take God's blessings for granted is to deny Him the praise and glory that He deserves and commands.

Because America is a land of religious freedom and tolerance, it has become a melting pot, not only of people, but also of faiths. We Americans are free to worship God as we see fit, but worship Him we must. Otherwise, we will stray from God's will and, in doing so, put ourselves—and our nation—in grave danger.

Today and every day, may we praise God through our words and our deeds, both as individuals and as a nation. When we do, we will surely remain one nation, blessed beyond measure, and watched over by a loving and merciful God.

The sacred writings tell us that "except the Lord builds the House, they labor in vain that build it." I therefore beg that henceforth prayers imploring the assistance of heaven, and its blessings on our deliberations, will be held in this Assembly every morning before we proceed to business.

Ben Franklin
(Philadelphia Constitutional Convention, 1787)

Throughout history, the presence and the power of prayer in the lives of righteous men and women have borne testimony to the dependence of mankind on a benevolent, caring God.

Jim Gallery

Do not pray for easy lives. Pray to be stronger men.

John F. Kennedy

As we join together in prayer, we draw on God's enabling might in a way that multiplies our own efforts many times over.

Shirley Dobson

Dear Lord,

America is my home, a land that
You have blessed beyond measure.
You have poured out Your blessings
on this nation, Lord; let me praise
You for Your glorious works. Today,
I pray for America, Father, that this
nation might follow Your Word and
Your will. Make this nation a land
of righteousness, courage, compassion,
and love for You.

Amen

2

One Nation Prays
FOR THOSE
WHO SERVE

The greatest among you will be your servant. For whoever exalts himself will be humbled, and whoever humbles himself will be exalted.

Matthew 23:11 NIV

The teachings of Jesus are crystal clear: We achieve greatness through service to others. But, as weak human beings, we sometimes fall short as we seek to puff ourselves up and glorify our own accomplishments. Jesus commands otherwise. If we seek spiritual greatness, we must first become servants. Jesus teaches that the most esteemed men and women are not the self-congratulatory leaders of society but are instead the humblest of servants.

Today, you may feel the temptation to build yourself up in the eyes of your neighbors. Resist that temptation. Instead, serve your neighbors quietly and without fanfare. Find a need and fill it . . . humbly. Lend a helping hand and share a word of kindness . . . anonymously. This is God's way.

Our nation needs not only your prayers but also your service. May you offer up both in a spirit of humility and thanksgiving.

And so, my fellow Americans, ask not what your country can do for you—ask what you can do for your country.

John F. Kennedy

In God's family, there is to be one great body of people: servants. In fact, that's the way to the top in his kingdom.

Chuck Swindoll

Some people give time, some give money, some their skills and connections, some literally give their life's blood. But everyone has something to give.

Barbara Bush

Everybody can be great because anybody can serve.

Martin Luther King, Jr.

Dear Lord,

In weak moments, I seek to build myself up by placing myself ahead of others. But, Your commandment, Father, is that I become a humble servant to those who need my encouragement, my help, and my love. Create in me a servant's heart. And, let me follow in the footsteps of Your Son who taught us by example that to be great in Your eyes, Lord, is to serve others humbly, faithfully, and lovingly.

Amen

3

One Nation Prays FOR OUR LEADERS

Obey your leaders and submit to their authority. They keep watch over you as men who must give an account.

Hebrews 13:17 NIV

*I*n his first letter to Timothy, Paul writes, "I urge, then, first of all, that requests, prayers, intercession and thanksgiving be made for everyone—for kings and all those in authority, that we may live peaceful and quiet lives in all godliness and holiness" (2:1-2 NIV). Paul's advice still applies; we must pray for everyone, including our leaders.

This generation of Americans faces problems that defy easy solutions, yet face them we must. We need leaders whose vision is clear and whose intentions are pure. In the Old Testament, Daniel writes, "Those who are wise will shine like the brightness of the heavens, and those who lead many to righteousness, like the stars for ever and ever" (*12:3 NIV*). Let us pray that our leaders will walk in wisdom as they direct us along the paths of righteousness.

It takes leaders with vision to help people with dreams.

Hubert H. Humphrey

We need to learn to set our course by the stars and not by the lights of every passing ship.

Omar Bradley

You can never separate a leader's actions from his character.

John Maxwell

Dear Lord,

I pray today for those who lead our country. Give them wisdom, courage, compassion, and faith. Today, I pray for those to whom You have entrusted the authority over this great nation. May they turn to You for guidance and for strength in all that they do.

Amen

4

One Nation Prays
FOR THOSE
WHO MOURN

Blessed are those who mourn, for they will be comforted.

Matthew 5:4 NIV

*G*rief is the price that life periodically exacts from those who live long and love deeply. When any of us experience a profound loss, darkness overwhelms us for a while, and it seems as if we cannot summon the strength to face another day— but, with God's help, we can. During times of heartache, we can turn to God, first for solace and then for renewal. When we do, He comforts us and, in time, He heals us.

Both as individual citizens and as a nation, we Americans mourn the loss of those who have paid the ultimate price for the freedoms we enjoy. Let us pray for their families. And, let us all seek the healing hand of our loving Father so that we might feel His comfort and His peace.

We cannot always understand the ways of Almighty God—the crosses which he sends us, the sacrifices which he demands of us. But, if we accept with faith and resignation his holy will—with no looking back to what might have been—we are at peace.

Rose Fitzgerald Kennedy

He who becomes a brother to the bruised, a doctor to the despairing, and a comforter to the crushed may not actually say much. What he has to offer is often beyond the power of speech to convey. But, the weary sense it, and it is a balm of Gilead to their souls.

Vance Havner

The grace of God is sufficient for all our needs, for every problem and for every difficulty, for every broken heart, and for every human sorrow.

Peter Marshall

Even in the winter, even in the midst of the storm, the sun is still there. Somewhere, up above the clouds, it still shines and warms and pulls at the life buried deep inside the brown branches and frozen earth. The sun is there! Spring will come.

Gloria Gaither

Dear Lord,

You have promised that You
will not give us more than we can bear;
You have promised to lift us out of our
grief and despair; You have promised to
put a new song on our lips. Today, Lord,
I pray for those who mourn, and I thank
You for sustaining all of us in our days
of sorrow. May we trust You always
and praise You forever.

Amen

5

One Nation Prays FOR GOD'S GUIDANCE

In his heart a man plans his course, but the Lord determines his steps.

Proverbs 16:9 NIV

*G*od has plans for our nation, but He won't force us to follow His will. To the contrary, He has given us free will, both as individuals and as a people. And, of course, with the freedom to choose comes the responsibility of living with the consequences of the choices we make.

Let us, as standard-bearers of the American Dream, seek guidance through the study of God's Word, and let us be watchful for His signs. God has richly blessed our nation, and He intends to use America in wonderful, unexpected ways. May we discover God's plan for our land, and may we follow it.

We have ample evidence that the Lord is able to guide. The promises cover every imaginable situation. All we need to do is to take the hand he stretches out.

Elisabeth Elliot

Make my path sure, O Lord. Establish my goings. Send me when and where You will and manifest to all that Thou are my guide.

Jim Elliot

It's a bit like river rafting with an experienced guide. You may panic when the guide steers you straight into a steep waterfall, especially if another course appears much safer. Yet, after you've emerged from the swirling depths and wiped the spray from your eyes, you see that just beyond the seemingly "safe" route was a series of jagged rocks. Your guide knew what he was doing after all.

Shirley Dobson

Men give advice; God gives guidance.

Leonard Ravenhill

Dear Lord,

I am Your creation, and You created me for a reason. Give me the wisdom to follow Your direction for my life's journey, and give our leaders the wisdom to direct our nation according to Your infinite wisdom and Your perfect will. Lead us, Father, and let us trust You completely, today and forever.

Amen

6

One Nation Prays
FOR PEACE

God has called us to live in peace.

1 Corinthians 7:15 NIV

As a godly nation, we seek peace, but not peace at all costs. When our nation is threatened, we must defend it or risk losing the liberties that we hold dear. Yet, even when we struggle against forces that would destroy us, we pray for the ultimate victory: lasting peace.

The beautiful words of John 14:27 give us hope: "Peace I leave with you, my peace I give unto you . . . ." We, as believers, can accept God's peace or ignore it. When we invite the peace of God into our lives, we are transformed. And then, because we possess the gift of peace, we can share that gift with fellow believers and with fellow citizens of all faiths.

Today, as a gift to yourself, to your family, to your friends, and to your nation, pray for peace in the world and for peace within your soul. Then, claim the inner peace that is your spiritual birthright: the peace that God intends for your life. It is offered freely; it has been paid for in full; it is yours for the asking. So ask. And then share.

Our first, our greatest, our most relentless purpose is peace. For without peace there is nothing.

Adlai E. Stevenson

It is neither wealth nor splendor, but tranquility and occupation, which give happiness.

Thomas Jefferson

A great many people are trying to make peace, but that has already been done. God has not left it for us to do; all we have to do is to enter into it.

D. L. Moody

God loves you and wants you to experience peace and life—abundant and eternal.

Billy Graham

Dear Lord,

You offer a peace that is perfect and
eternal. Let me turn the cares and
burdens of my life over to You, and
let me feel the spiritual abundance
that You offer. Today, I also pray for
peace among nations, Father, and
for brotherly love among Your children
throughout the world. You are the
source of peace, Dear Lord;
let us find it in You.

Amen

7

One Nation Prays FOR GOD'S BLESSINGS

I will make you into a great nation and I will bless you; I will make your name great, and you will be a blessing. I will bless those who bless you, and whoever curses you I will curse; and all peoples on earth will be blessed through you.

Genesis 12:2-3 NIV

*I*f we sit down and begin counting the blessings that God has bestowed upon our nation, the list is improbably long. At the top of that list, of course, is the priceless gift of freedom: the freedom to live, vote, work, and worship without fear. God has also blessed America with unsurpassed material wealth; we are, in fact, the most prosperous nation in the history of humanity.

As believers, we must never take God's blessings for granted. Instead, we must give thanks to the Giver for the gifts that He has given us.

To those to whom much is given, much is expected, and so it is with America. We are the world's superpower, and as such, we have profound responsibilities to our own citizens and, to a lesser extent, to those who live beyond our borders. The challenges are great, and no single individual, no matter how wise, can chart the proper course for our nation. But, *we the people*—under God and respectful of His commandments—*can* join together to protect and preserve our nation and, in doing so, give protection and hope to freedom-loving people around the globe.

God wants his people to earnestly seek his will and to pray for it, and thus to become agents of the blessing God brings.

James Montgomery Boice

The God who gave us life gave us liberty at the same time.

Thomas Jefferson

Jesus intended for us to be overwhelmed by the blessings of regular days. He said it was the reason he had come: "I am come that they might have life, and that they might have it more abundantly."

Gloria Gaither

When God blesses us, He expects us to use those blessings to bless the lives of others.

Mary Prince

Dear Lord,

You have given me so much, and I am thankful. Today, I seek Your continued blessings for my life, for my family, and for my nation. Let me share Your gifts with others, and let my nation show generosity to people throughout the world. We are blessed that we might bless others. Let us give thanks for Your gifts . . . and let us share them.

Amen

8

One Nation Prays FOR COURAGE IN ADVERSITY

God is our refuge and strength, an ever-present help in trouble.

Psalm 46:1 NIV

The American Dream was forged on the anvil of adversity. Tough times are nothing new to the American people: we began facing and overcoming adversity long before John Hancock proudly penned his name on the Declaration of Independence. Through wars, epidemics, social unrest, and economic distress, Americans have faced their problems and risen above them. And so it is today.

As we begin the 21st century, the world is indeed a dangerous place. But through adversity, we grow stronger. Abigail Adams said it well, "It is not in the still calm of life, or in repose of pacific station that great characters are formed . . . Great necessities call our great virtues."

Giving up or becoming discouraged is not the answer to difficult times. The times that try men's souls are also the times when wise men and women turn to God in prayer. E.M. Bounds writes, "God shapes the world by prayer. The more praying there is in the world, the better the world will be, and the mightier will be the forces against evil." Today, as in years gone by, America will grow stronger as we turn to the Creator of the universe for the victory that only He can provide.

It is part of the American character to consider nothing as desperate, to surmount every difficulty by resolution and contrivance.

Thomas Jefferson

Oftentimes God demonstrates His faithfulness in adversity by providing for us what we need to survive. He does not change our painful circumstances. He sustains us through them.

Chuck Swindoll

No time is too hard for God, no situation too difficult.

Norman Vincent Peale

Down through the centuries, in times of trouble and trial, God has brought courage to the hearts of those who love Him. The Bible is filled with assurances of God's help and comfort in every kind of trouble which might cause fears to arise in the human heart. You can look ahead with promise, hope, and joy.

Billy Graham

Dear Lord,

We give You thanks in all
circumstances. And, when we face
the inevitable challenges and difficulties
of life, we turn to You. When we
encounter situations that we cannot
understand, we trust in You. You are
the Creator and sovereign God.
And we give the glory and the thanks
to You, God, for the ultimate
victory that You have promised
Your faithful children.

Amen

9

One Nation Prays FOR UNITY

Every kingdom divided against itself will be ruined, and every city or household divided against itself will not stand.

Matthew 12:25 NIV

"*One* nation, under God, indivisible . . . ." We have heard these words on countless occasions, and yet, amid the din of partisanship, we sometimes forget that if America is to remain strong, we, her citizens, must remain united.

We should never confuse unity with unanimity. As men and women of good faith, Americans inevitably disagree about matters of policy. But, we Americans must never allow our differences of opinion to obscure the fact that ours is a great nation precisely *because* of our disagreements. We are a diverse nation composed of independently minded citizens who, because of our collective liberties, are free to think and speak as we see fit. Thankfully, we can do so without fear.

Amid the inevitable disagreements that are part of the grand American debate, we must never sacrifice our unity of purpose: the sincere desire to leave a better nation to the next generation than the one we received from the last. Today, let us pray for America that she might remain free, united, and strong: one nation under God, with liberty and justice for all.

Let it be borne on the flag under which we rally in every exigency, that we have one country, one constitution, one destiny.

Daniel Webster

Our strength is our unity of purpose. To that high concept, there can be no end save victory.

Franklin D. Roosevelt

The government is the strongest of which every man feels himself a part.

Thomas Jefferson

There is no power on earth equal to the power of free men and women united in the bonds of human brotherhood.

Walter P. Reuther

Dear Lord,

So much more can be accomplished when we join together to fulfill our common goals and desires. As I seek to fulfill Your will for my life, let me also join with others to accomplish Your greater good for our nation and for all humanity.

Amen

10

One Nation Prays FOR TOLERANCE AND UNDERSTANDING

Now we see but a poor reflection as in a mirror;
then we shall see face to face. Now I know in part;
then I shall know fully, even as I am fully known.

1 Corinthians 13:12 NIV

The words of Jesus are unambiguous: "Do not judge, and you will not be judged. Do not condemn, and you will not be condemned. Forgive, and you will be forgiven" (Luke 6:37-38 NIV). And yet, because we are fallible human beings, we are often quick to judge others. The irony of our judgments, of course, is that we, too, have fallen short of God's commandments, and we often seek pardon for ourselves (even if we fail to grant it to others).

America is a land of tolerance; we Americans are a forgiving people. May it always be so. As Christian believers, we are warned that to judge others is to invite fearful consequences: to the extent we judge others, so, too, will we be judged by God. Let us refrain, then, from judging our neighbors; let us seek, instead, to understand them and, when necessary, let us be quick to forgive them—just as God has already forgiven us.

I hope ever to see America among the foremost nations in examples of justice and tolerance.

George Washington

No loss by flood and lightning, no destruction of cities and temples by the hostile forces of nature, has deprived man of so many noble lives and impulses as those which intolerance has destroyed.

Helen Keller

The spirit of liberty is the spirit which seeks to understand the minds of other men and women; the spirit of liberty is the spirit which weighs their interest alongside its own without bias.

Learned Hand

If you seek to teach your countrymen tolerance, you yourself must be tolerant; if you would teach them liberality for the opinions of others, you yourself must be liberal; and if you would teach them unselfish patriotism, you yourself must be unselfish and patriotic.

Grover Cleveland

Dear Lord,

Sometimes I am quick to judge others. But, You have commanded me not to judge. Keep me mindful, Father, that when I judge others, I am living outside of Your will for my life. You have forgiven me, Lord. Let me forgive others, let me love them, and let me help them . . . without judging them.

Amen

11

One Nation Prays FOR DELIVERANCE FROM EVIL

Even though I walk through the valley of the shadow of death, I will fear no evil, for you are with me; your rod and your staff, they comfort me.

Psalm 23:4 NIV

*I*n his letter to Jewish Christians who had been driven out of Jerusalem, Peter offered a stern warning: "Your adversary, the devil, prowls around like a roaring lion, seeking someone to devour" (I Peter 5:8 NASB). What was true in New Testament times is equally true in our own. Satan tempts his prey and then seeks to devour them.

As believers, we must beware, and as Americans, we must be vigilant. Evil is indeed abroad in the world, and Satan continues to sow the seeds of destruction far and wide. If we seek righteousness in our own lives *and* in the collective life of our nation, we must earnestly wrap ourselves in the protection of God's Holy Word. When we do, we are secure.

The world is a dangerous place to live, not because of the people who are evil, but because of the people who don't do anything about it.

Albert Einstein

There are a thousand hacking at the branches of evil to one who is striking at the root.

Henry David Thoreau

God shapes the world by prayer. The more praying there is in the world, the better the world will be, and the mightier will be the forces against evil.

E. M. Bounds

We are in a continual battle with the spiritual forces of evil, but we will triumph when we yield to God's leading and call on His powerful presence in prayer.

Shirley Dobson

Dear Lord,

Strengthen my walk with You.
Evil can devour me, and it comes in
so many disguises. Sometimes, Father,
I need Your help to recognize right from
wrong. Your presence in my life enables
me to choose truth and to live a life that
is pleasing to You. May I always live in
Your presence, and may I walk with
You today . . . and forever.

Amen

12

One Nation Prays
FOR TRUST IN GOD

It is better to trust in the LORD than to put confidence in man. It is better to trust in the LORD than to put confidence in princes.

Psalm 118:8-9 KJV

*D*o you seek God's blessings for yourself and your family? Then trust Him. Trust Him with every aspect of your life. Trust Him with your relationships. Trust Him with your finances. Follow His commandments and pray for His guidance. Then, wait patiently for God's revelations and for His blessings. In His own fashion and in His own time, God will bless you in ways that you never could have imagined.

Do you seek God's blessings for America? Then pray for our nation. Pray that we, as a people, trust God and follow His Word. If we do, we will continue to receive the blessings that God has so richly bestowed upon us and upon our nation.

Then conquer we must, when our cause it is just, and this be our motto: "In God is our Trust!"

Francis Scott Key

Ours is not only a fortunate people but a very practical people, with vision high but with their feet on the earth, with belief in themselves and with faith in God.

Warren G. Harding

God is God. He knows what he is doing. When you can't trace his hand, trust his heart.

Max Lucado

Trust in yourself and you are doomed to disappointment; trust in money and you may have it taken from you, but trust in God, and you are never to be confounded in time or eternity.

D. L. Moody

Dear Lord,

When I trust in things of this earth,
I will be disappointed. But, when I put
my faith in You, I am secure. You are my
rock and my shield. Upon Your firm
foundation I will build my life. When I
am worried, Lord, let me trust in You.
You will love me and protect me, and
You will share Your boundless grace
today, tomorrow, and forever.

Amen

13

One Nation Prays
FOR THE WILL
TO PERSEVERE

You need to persevere so that when you have done the will of God, you will receive what he has promised.

Hebrews 10:36 NIV

As Americans living in a difficult and dangerous world, we know that the key to success, both as individuals and as a nation, is often nothing more than a willingness to persevere. Sometimes, however, when the storm clouds form overhead and we find ourselves in the dark valley of despair, our faith is stretched to the breaking point. But, as believers, we can be comforted: Wherever we find ourselves, whether at the top of the mountain or in the depths of the valley, God is there. And, because He cares for us, we can live courageously.

The next time you find your courage tested to the limit, remember that God is as near as your next breath, and remember that He offers strength and comfort to His children. He is your shield and your strength; He is your protector and your deliverer. Call upon Him in your hour of need and then be comforted. Whatever your challenge, whatever your trouble, God can help you persevere. And will.

When you get into a tight place and everything goes against you, till it seems as though you could not hang on a minute longer, never give up then, for that is just the place and the time the tide will turn.

Harriet Beecher Stowe

Stand still and refuse to retreat. Look at it as God looks at it and draw upon his power to hold up under the blast.

Chuck Swindoll

In the Bible, patience is not a passive acceptance of circumstances. It is a courageous perseverance in the face of suffering and difficulty.

Warren Wiersbe

Genius is divine perseverance. Genius I cannot claim, nor even extra brightness, but perseverance all can have.

Woodrow Wilson

Dear Lord,

When the pace of my life becomes
frantic, slow me down and give me
perspective. And Father, when
the pace of world events spins
ever faster, keep America's leaders
steady and sure. Give them courage,
perseverance, and wisdom so that,
as a nation, we Americans might
remain one nation, under God . . .
forever.

Amen

14

One Nation Prays WITH THANKFUL HEARTS

Rejoice evermore. Pray without ceasing. In every thing give thanks: for this is the will of God in Christ Jesus concerning you.

1 Thessalonians 5:16-18 KJV

When we honor God and place Him at the center of our lives, every day is a cause for thanksgiving and celebration. God fills each day to the brim with possibilities, and He challenges us to use our lives for His purposes.

Every morning at dawn, the sun breaks over the Atlantic Ocean on a land of freedom and opportunity. The new day is presented to us free of charge, but we must beware: Today is a nonrenewable resource—once it's gone, it's gone forever. Our responsibility—both as Americans and believers—is to use this day in the service of God's will and in the service of His people.

Each new day is an opportunity to thank the Giver for His gifts. May we do so with our words, with our prayers, with our thoughts, and with our deeds.

The unthankful heart discovers no mercies, but the thankful heart finds, in every hour, some heavenly blessings.

Henry Ward Beecher

When it comes to life, the critical thing is whether you take things for granted or take them with gratitude.

G. K. Chesterton

God is in control, and therefore in everything I can give thanks, not because of the situation, but because of the One who directs and rules over it.

Kay Arthur

It is only with gratitude that life becomes rich.

Dietrich Bonhoeffer

Dear Lord,

Your gifts are greater than I can imagine.
May I live each day with thanksgiving
in my heart and praise on my lips.
Thank You for the gift of Your Son
and for the promise of eternal life.
Let me share the joyous news of
Jesus Christ, and let my life be
a testimony to His love
and His grace.

Amen

15

One Nation Prays TO KNOW GOD'S WILL AND HIS WORD

Your word is a lamp to my feet and a light for my path.

Psalm 119:105 NIV

These are difficult days in America. We are faced with challenges—both from inside our borders and from outside them—that are new to this generation. In difficult times such as these, we learn lessons that we could have learned in no other way: we learn about life, but more importantly, we learn about ourselves. Adversity visits everyone—no human being is beyond Old Man Trouble's reach. Old Man Trouble is not only an unwelcome guest, but he is also an invaluable teacher. If we are to become mature human beings, it is our duty to learn from the inevitable hardships and heartbreaks of life.

When we trust God completely, we have every reason to live courageously. God is in His heaven, we are His children, and He is in control. May we follow His Word and seek His will, knowing that faith in the Father is the immovable cornerstone in the foundation of courageous living.

The Bible is the Rock on which this Republic rests.

Andrew Jackson

All the good from the Savior of the world is communicated through this Book, the Bible; but for the Book we could not know right from wrong. All the things desirable to man are contained in it.

Abraham Lincoln

It is impossible to rightly govern the world without God and the Bible. Do not ever let anyone claim to be a true American patriot if they ever attempt to separate religion from politics.

George Washington

The purpose of all prayer is to find God's will and to make that will our prayer.

Catherine Marshall

Dear Lord,

As I journey through this life help me
always to consult the true road map:
Your Holy Word. I know that when
I turn my heart and my thoughts to
You, Father, You will lead me along
the path that is right for me. And, when
our nation's leaders seek Your will,
they, too, will discover the wisdom of
Your Holy Word. Today, dear Lord,
let me know Your will and study Your
Word, and let America's leaders fulfill
Your plan for our nation.

Amen

16

One Nation Prays
WITH HOPE AND
ASSURANCE

Happy is he…whose hope is in the LORD his God.

Psalm 146:5 KJV

When a suffering woman sought healing by merely touching the hem of His cloak, Jesus replied, "Daughter, be of good comfort; thy faith hath made thee whole" (Matthew 9:22 KJV). The message to believers is clear: if we are to be made whole by God, we must live by faith. But, when we face adversity, anxiety, or heartbreak, living by faith can be difficult indeed. Still, God remains faithful to us, and we should remain faithful to Him.

Today's generation of Americans faces challenges and dangers that are unique to this time in world history. But, one thing remains unchanged: we still need God. Today, let us pray for faith and courage. Let us live out this day—and every one thereafter—with an unwavering trust in God. When we do, we will be made whole.

Great hopes make great men.

Thomas Fuller

Earth's best is only a dim reflection and a preliminary rendering of the glory that will one day be revealed.

Joni Eareckson Tada

When you accept the fact that sometimes seasons are dry and times are hard and that God is in control of both, you will discover a sense of divine refuge because the hope then is in God and not in yourself.

Chuck Swindoll

Hope! What a wonderful word it is! Write it indelibly on your mind. H-O-P-E. It is a bright word, shining and scintillating and dynamic, forward looking, full of courage and optimism. With this word, let us begin tomorrow.

Norman Vincent Peale

Dear Lord,

Today I will trust Your will
for my life, for my family, and for
my nation. If I become discouraged,
I will turn to You. If I grow weary,
I will seek strength in You. And,
may the leaders of America also
turn to You, dear God, in these
turbulent times. You are our God
and our salvation; let us place
our hopes and our faith in You.

Amen

17

One Nation Prays

FOR THOSE WHO SUFFER AROUND THE WORLD

Weeping may endure for a night, but joy cometh in the morning.

Psalm 30:5 KJV

How fortunate we are to live in a land of opportunities and possibilities. But, for many people around the world, opportunities are scarce at best. In too many corners of the globe, hardworking men and women struggle mightily to provide food and shelter for their families.

The man from Galilee advised His followers, "I tell you the truth, whatever you did for one of the least of these brothers of mine, you did for me" (Matthew 25:40 NIV). Jesus' words still apply. When we care for the downtrodden, we follow in the footsteps of Christ. And, when we show compassion for those who suffer, we abide by the commandments of the One who created us. May we Americans hear the Word of God . . . and follow it.

Although the world is full of suffering, it is also full of overcoming it.

Helen Keller

We must build a new world, a far better world—one in which the eternal dignity of man is respected.

Harry S Truman

The Bible is a Christian's guidebook, and I believe the knowledge it sheds on pain and suffering is the great antidote to fear for suffering people. Knowledge can dissolve fear as light destroys darkness.

Philip Yancey

To those peoples in the huts and villages across the globe struggling to break the bonds of mass misery, we pledge our best efforts to help them to help themselves.

John F. Kennedy

Dear Lord,

Keep me mindful that every man
and woman, every boy and girl is
Your child. Let me give to the needy,
let me pray for those who mourn,
and let me care for those who suffer.
And, Father, let this great nation be
a symbol of generosity and caring
to needy people throughout
the world.

Amen

18

One Nation Prays FOR OUR FAMILIES

...these should learn first of all to put their religion into practice by caring for their own family....

1 Timothy 5:4 NIV

These are difficult days for our nation and for our families. But, thankfully, God is bigger than all of our challenges. God loves us and protects us. In times of trouble, he comforts us; in times of sorrow, He dries our tears. When we are troubled, or weak, or sorrowful, God is as near as our next breath.

Are you concerned for the wellbeing of your family? You are not alone. We live in a world where temptation and danger seem to lurk on every street corner. Parents and children alike have good reason to be watchful. But, despite the evils of our time, God remains steadfast. Let us build our lives on the rock that cannot be shaken…let us trust in our Creator. Even in these difficult days, no problem is too big for God.

Whatever the times, one thing will never change: If you have children, they must come first. Your success as a family and our success as a society depends not on what happens in the White House, but on what happens inside your house.

Barbara Bush

Many of the most highly publicized events of my presidency are not nearly as memorable or significant in my life as fishing with my daddy.

Jimmy Carter

The only true source of meaning in life is found in love for God and his son Jesus Christ, and love for mankind, beginning with our own families.

James Dobson

Money can build or buy a house. Add love to that, and you have a home. Add God to that, and you have a temple. You have "a little colony of the kingdom of heaven."

Anne Ortland

Dear Lord,

I am blessed to be part of the family
of God where I find love and
acceptance. You have also blessed
me with my earthly family. Today
I pray for them and for all the families
in America and for families throughout
our world. Protect us and guide us,
Lord. And, as I reach out to my own
family, may I show them the same love
and care that You have shown to me.

Amen

19

One Nation Prays FOR WISDOM AND PERSPECTIVE

Blessed is the man who finds wisdom, the man who gains understanding….

Proverbs 3:13 NIV

*W*isdom is built slowly over a lifetime. It is the sum of every right decision and every honorable deed. It requires the willingness to learn from past mistakes and the faith to seek God's will in decisions both great and small. Wisdom results from countless hours spent in heartfelt prayer. It is forged on the anvil of honorable work and polished by the twin virtues of generosity and humility. Wisdom is a priceless thing, and in today's fast-changing world, America needs it desperately.

Perspective, too, is a precious commodity, one that is often in short supply, especially during difficult days. Today, let us pray for our leaders, that they might possess the insight and the judgment to direct our nation during this time of adversity and change. And, may God grant us, this generation of American citizens, the collective wisdom to select our leaders wisely and the courage to protect our freedoms vigorously.

Don't expect wisdom to come into your life like great chunks of rock on a conveyor belt. Wisdom comes privately from God as a byproduct of right decisions, godly reactions, and the application of spiritual principles to daily circumstances.

Chuck Swindoll

If you lack knowledge, go to school. If you lack wisdom, get on your knees.

Vance Havner

Earthly fears are no fears at all. Answer the big question of eternity, and the little questions of life fall into perspective.

Max Lucado

The next time you're faced with tough times, ask yourself if this is a problem that will concern you on your deathbed. If not, don't disturb yourself too much.

Criswell Freeman

Dear Lord,

Sometimes, amid the trials of
the moment, even the wisest men
and women may lose perspective.
Today I pray for America's leaders.
Give them divine guidance, and lead
them according to Your will. And,
keep all our citizens ever mindful that
Your reality is the ultimate reality, and
that Your wisdom is the ultimate
wisdom, now and forever.

Amen

20

One Nation Prays
WITH PRAISE FOR THE CREATOR

I will thank you, Lord, in front of all the people. I will sing your praises among the nations. For your unfailing love is higher than the heavens. Your faithfulness reaches to the clouds.

Psalm 108:3-4 NLT

When we honor God and place Him at the center of our lives, every day is a cause for celebration. God fills each day to the brim with possibilities, and He challenges us to use our lives for His purposes. Every morning, the sun rises over a land of freedom and opportunity.

Today, let us praise God for His blessings, and let us show our gratitude not only through our prayers, but, more importantly, through our deeds.

No part of our prayers creates a greater feeling of joy than when we praise God for who He is. He is our Master Creator, our Father, our source of all love.

Shirley Dobson

Preoccupy my thoughts with your praise beginning today.

Joni Eareckson Tada

How delightful a teacher, but gentle a provider, how bountiful a giver is my Father! Praise, praise to Thee, O manifested Most High.

Jim Elliot

Praise and thank God for who He is and for what He has done for you.

Billy Graham

Dear Lord,

Your hand created the smallest grain
of sand and the grandest stars in the
heavens. You watch over Your entire
creation, and You watch over me.
Thank You, Lord, for loving this
world so much that You sent Your
Son to die for our sins. Let me always
be grateful for the priceless gift of
Your Son, and let me praise
Your Holy name forever.

Amen

21

One Nation Prays FOR JUSTICE

He has showed you, O man, what is good. And what does the LORD require of you? To act justly and to love mercy and to walk humbly with your God.

Micah 6:8 NIV

The Pledge of Allegiance concludes with words that comfort and reassure us: ". . . with liberty and justice for all." As freedom-loving Americans, we must seek justice not only for ourselves but also for our fellow citizens *and* for those around the world.

Thankfully, America remains a nation dedicated to the principle of equal justice for all its citizens. May we, as modern-day patriots, commit ourselves to lives characterized by truth and justice. And, let us pray that America remains a land of liberty for all of her people.

Justice, sir, is the great interest of man on earth. It is the ligament which holds civilized beings and civilized nations together.

Daniel Webster

Man is unjust, but God is just, and finally justice triumphs.

Henry Wadsworth Longfellow

The answer to injustice is not to silence the critic but to end the injustice.

Paul Robeson

I believe in one God, and no more, and I hope for happiness beyond this life. I believe in the equality of man; and I believe that religious duties consist in doing justice, loving mercy, and endeavoring to make our fellow creatures happy.

Thomas Paine

Dear Lord,

You have told us to love mercy,
to walk humbly with You, and
to act justly. Father, help me this day
to be just in all my personal dealings,
and, in some small way, to seek
justice for all mankind.

Amen

22

One Nation Prays
FOR RENEWAL AND STRENGTH

Those who hope in the LORD will renew their strength. They will soar on wings like eagles; they will run and not grow weary, they will walk and not be faint.

Isaiah 40:31 NIV

For many Americans, these are difficult days indeed. Adversity, of course, visits everyone in time—no one is exempt. And, when difficult times arrive, we may become discouraged or worse. Thankfully, there is a source from which we can draw the power needed to renew our strength. That source is God.

God intends that His children lead joyous lives filled with abundance and peace. But sometimes, abundance and peace seem very far away. It is then that we must turn to God for renewal, and when we do, He will restore us.

Are you tired or troubled? Turn your heart toward God in prayer. Are you weak or worried? Take the time to delve deeply into God's Holy Word. Are you spiritually depleted? Call upon fellow believers to support you, and call upon God to renew your spirit and your life. When you do, you'll discover that the Creator of the universe stands always ready and always able to create a new sense of wonder and joy in you.

God is not running an antique shop! He is making all things new!

Vance Havner

God is the One who provides our strength, not only to cope with the demands of the day, but also to rise above them. May we look to Him for the strength to soar.

Jim Gallery

Prayer plumes the wings of God's young eaglets so that they may learn to mount above the clouds. Prayer brings inner strength to God's warriors and sends them forth to spiritual battle with their muscles firm and their armor in place.

C. H. Spurgeon

Do not pray for easy lives. Pray to be stronger men! Do not pray for tasks equal to your powers. Pray for powers equal to your tasks.

Phillips Brooks

Dear Lord,

Sometimes I am troubled, and
sometimes I grow weary. When
I am weak, Lord, give me strength.
When I am discouraged, renew me.
When I am fearful, let me feel Your
healing touch. Let me always trust in
Your promises, Lord, and let me draw
strength from those promises and
from Your unending love.

Amen

23

One Nation Prays FOR A SPIRIT OF FORGIVENESS

For if you forgive men when they sin against
you, your heavenly Father will also forgive you.

Matthew 6:14-15 NIV

Forgiveness is God's commandment, but oh how difficult a commandment it can be to follow. Being frail, fallible, imperfect human beings, we are quick to anger, quick to blame, slow to forgive, and even slower to forget. No matter. Forgiveness is God's way, and it must be our way, too.

God's Holy Word is a book that must be taken in its entirety; all of God's commandments are to be taken seriously. And, so it is with forgiveness.

If, in your heart, you hold bitterness against even a single person, forgive. If there exists even one person, alive or dead, whom you have not forgiven, follow God's commandment and His will for your life: forgive. If you are embittered against yourself for some past mistake or shortcoming, forgive. Then, to the best of your abilities, forget. And move on. For individual citizens *and* for great nations like America, the time to forgive is now.

Develop and maintain the capacity to forgive.

Martin Luther King, Jr.

When God tells us to love our enemies, he gives, along with the command, the love itself.

Corrie ten Boom

Looking back over my life, all I can see is mercy and grace written in large letters everywhere. May God help me have the same kind of heart toward those who wound or offend me.

Jim Cymbala

There is no revenge so complete as forgiveness.

Josh Billings

Dear Lord,

When I am bitter, You can change
my unforgiving heart. And,
when I am slow to forgive,
Your Word reminds me that
forgiveness is Your commandment.
Let me be Your obedient servant,
Lord, and let me forgive others just as
You have forgiven me. And, Father,
give the leaders of our nation a spirit
of forgiveness and reconciliation
so that America might be
an instrument of Your will
here on earth.

Amen

24

One Nation Prays FOR RIGHTEOUS HEARTS

Blessed are those who hunger and thirst for righteousness, for they will be filled.

Matthew 5:6 NIV

God has given us a guidebook for righteous living called the Holy Bible. It contains thorough instructions which, if followed, lead to fulfillment, righteousness, and joy. But, if we choose to ignore God's commandments, either as individuals or as a nation, the results are as predictable as they are tragic.

A righteous life has many components: faith, honesty, generosity, love, kindness, humility, gratitude, and worship, to name but a few. If we seek to receive the blessings that the Father intends for our lives and for our country, we must live righteously and according to the principles contained in God's Holy Word. And, for further instructions, read the manual.

Let us have faith that right makes might, and in that faith, let us dare to do our duty as we understand it.

Abraham Lincoln

A life growing in its purity and devotion will be a more prayerful life.

E. M. Bounds

We must appropriate the tender mercy of God every day after conversion, or problems quickly develop. We need his grace daily in order to live a righteous life.

Jim Cymbala

Our progress in holiness depends on God and ourselves—on God's grace and on our will to be holy.

Mother Teresa

Dear Lord,

I pray that America might remain
a righteous nation, and I pray that I,
too, might live according to Your
commandments. When I take my
eye away from You and Your Word,
I suffer. But, when I turn my thoughts,
my faith, my trust, and my prayers to
You, Heavenly Father, You guide my
path. Let me live righteously according
to Your commandments, and let me
discover Your will and follow Your
Word this day and always.

Amen

25

One Nation Prays
FOR A SPIRIT OF
GENEROSITY

Freely you have received, freely give.

Matthew 10:8 NIV

*S*ince its earliest days, America has truly been "one nation, under God." And, the Word of God instructs us that service to others is one way of fulfilling His purpose here on earth. Romans 12:10 reminds us, "Be devoted to one another in brotherly love" (NIV). Thankfully, Americans of every generation have heeded these words.

We live in a world in which too many people must struggle to obtain the basic necessities of life. As Americans, we have been richly blessed, and we must be quick to share our blessings. Whether the needs are here at home or far away, the response is the same: we, as responsible citizens of the most prosperous nation on earth, must care enough to help.

The highest test of the civilization of any race is in its willingness to extend a helping hand to the less fortunate. A race, like an individual, lifts itself up by lifting others up.

Booker T. Washington

No person was ever honored for what he received. Honor has been the reward for what he gave.

Calvin Coolidge

He climbs the highest who helps another up.

Zig Ziglar

What is serving God? 'Tis doing good to man.

Poor Richard's Almanac

Dear Lord,

Your gifts are beyond comprehension.
You gave Your Son Jesus to save us,
and Your motivation was love. I pray
that the gifts I give to others will come
from an overflow of my heart, and
that they will echo the great love You
have for all of Your children.

Amen

26

One Nation Prays
FOR FREEDOM

Where the Spirit of the Lord is, there is freedom.

2 Corinthians 3:17 NIV

Abraham Lincoln's words still ring true: "No man is good enough to govern another man without the other's consent." But, across the globe, tyranny and oppression still grip the lives of far too many innocent men, women, and children. When people anywhere are denied their freedoms, people everywhere are threatened. And so it is that American men and women must, on occasion, travel far beyond our borders to protect the lives and liberties of foreign citizens.

Perhaps you have sometimes taken America's freedoms for granted. If so, welcome to the club. In a land so richly blessed, it is easy to forget how hard our forefathers struggled to earn the blessings that we enjoy today. But, we must never forget, and we must never become complacent.

In America, no man governs alone. We the people make the laws, enforce the laws, and change the laws when those laws need changing. For these liberties, we must thank those who have gone before us *and* our Father who reigns above us. And, the best way to say "thank you" for our blessings is to defend them, whatever the cost.

Freedom is the last, best hope of earth.

Abraham Lincoln

Everything that is really good and inspiring is created by individuals who labor in freedom.

Albert Einstein

All men are born free and equal, and have certain natural, essential, and unalienable rights.

Constitution of Massachusetts

If it be the pleasure of Heaven that my country shall require the poor offering of my life, the victim shall be ready, at the appointed hour of sacrifice, come when that hour may. But while I do live, let me have a country that is free.

John Adams

Dear Lord,

Thank You for this nation and
for the freedoms we enjoy here.
Give us the courage to preserve
our precious liberties and
the strength to share them with
oppressed people around the world.
May we speak out against injustice and
oppression of any kind…anywhere.
And, may the flame of freedom that
burns brightly here in America be a
beacon for all the world to see.

Amen

27

One Nation Prays
FOR OUR CHILDREN

Train a child in the way he should go, and when he is old he will not turn from it.

Proverbs 22:6 NIV

*O*ur children are this nation's most precious resource. And, as responsible adults, we must create a homeland in which the next generation of Americans can live in safety and in freedom. Thankfully, the American Dream is alive and well; it is our responsibility to ensure that it remains so. We must protect our nation's liberties with the same sense of dedication and urgency that our forebears demonstrated when they earned those liberties on the fields of battle and in the halls of justice.

Today, let us pray for our children . . . *all* of them. Let us pray for children here at home *and* for children around the world. Every child is God's child. May we, as concerned adults, behave—and pray—accordingly.

O Lord…build me a son whose heart will be clear, whose goal will be high, a son who will master himself before he seeks to master other men; one who will reach into the future, yet never forget the past.

Douglas MacArthur

Praying for our children is a noble task. There is nothing more special, more precious, than time that a parent spends struggling and pondering with God on behalf of a child.

Max Lucado

Let's please God by actively seeking, through prayer, "peaceful and quiet lives" for ourselves, our spouses, our children and grandchildren, our friends, and our nation (1 Timothy 2:1-3 NIV).

Shirley Dobson

I have a dream that my four little children will one day live in a nation where they will not be judged by the color of their skin, but by the content of their character.

Martin Luther King, Jr.

Dear Lord,

The children of this world are
Your children. Let us love them,
care for them, nurture them,
teach them, and lead them to You.
And today, as I serve as an example
to the children under my care, let my
words and deeds demonstrate the love
that I feel for them . . . and for You.

Amen

28

One Nation Prays
FOR PATIENCE

Wait patiently on the Lord. Be brave and courageous. Yes, wait patiently on the Lord.

Psalm 27:14 NLT

As individuals and as a nation, we become impatient for the changes that we so earnestly desire. We want solutions to our problems, and we want them now! But sometimes, life's greatest challenges defy easy solutions, so we must be patient.

Psalm 37:7 commands us to wait patiently for God, but, for most of us, waiting quietly for Him is difficult. Why? Because we are fallible human beings who seek solutions to our problems today, if not sooner. We seek to manage our lives according to our own timetables, not God's. Still, God instructs us to be patient in all things, and that is as it should be. After all, think how patient God has been with us.

He that can have patience can have what he will.

Ben Franklin

All good abides with him who waits wisely.

Henry David Thoreau

Waiting means going about our assigned tasks, confident that God will provide the meaning and the conclusions.

Eugene Peterson

Let God use times of waiting to mold and shape your character. Let God use those times to purify your life and make you into a clean vessel for His service.

Henry Blackaby and Claude King

Dear Lord,

Make our nation a land of wisdom,
patience, and perseverance . . .
starting with me. Let me wait quietly
for You. May I live according to
Your plan and according to Your
timetable. When I am hurried,
slow me down. When I become
impatient with others, give me
empathy. Today, let me be a patient
servant as I trust in You, Father,
and in Your master plan.

Amen

29

One Nation Prays
FOR THOSE WHO LONG TO BE FREE

The Spirit of the Lord is on me, because he has anointed me to preach good news to the poor. He has sent me to proclaim freedom for the prisoners and recovery of sight for the blind, to release the oppressed, to proclaim the year of the Lord's favor.

Luke 4:18-19 NIV

We Americans have enjoyed our liberties for so long that sometimes we take them for granted. Others do not. All around the globe, hardworking men and women long to come to our shores and breathe the fresh air of freedom. While our nation cannot welcome all people who wish to make America their home, we *can* do our part to spread the gospel of freedom and justice throughout the world . . . and we should.

In his second letter to the church in Corinth, Paul writes, "Where the Spirit of the Lord is, there is freedom" (3:17 NIV). Today, let us pray for those people around the world who seek freedom, and let us do whatever we can to help them find it.

The aspiration toward freedom is the most essentially human of all human manifestations.

Eric Hoffer

America means opportunity, freedom, power.

Ralph Waldo Emerson

The bosom of America is open to receive not only the opulent and respectable stranger, but the oppressed and persecuted of all nations and religions, whom we shall welcome in participation of all our rights and privileges, if by decency and propriety of conduct they appear to merit the enjoyment.

George Washington

We become not a melting pot but a beautiful mosaic. Different people, different beliefs, different yearnings, different hopes, different dreams.

Jimmy Carter

Dear Lord,

You have blessed me with the
opportunity to live in a nation that
treasures freedom. I know that some
people in this world are not as fortunate.
Today, I pray for all humanity, especially
those who long to be free. May they find
the liberties that they so earnestly seek,
and may they live their lives in peace,
security, and happiness.

Amen

30

One Nation Prays
FOR GOD'S GRACE

My grace is sufficient for you, for my power is made perfect in weakness.

2 Corinthians 12:9 NIV

*N*one of us have earned the freedoms and opportunities that we enjoy here in America; those blessings are a cumulative bequest of our forebears and a priceless gift from God above. Today, let us pray that God continues to bless this nation and that His grace will touch the hearts of all our people.

Let us praise God for His gifts, and let us share His Word with all who cross our paths. God's grace is the ultimate gift, and we owe to Him the ultimate in thanksgiving. We demonstrate our thanks by sharing His message and His love.

Yes, God's grace is always sufficient, and His arms are always open to give it. But, will our arms be open to receive it?

Beth Moore

God shares himself generously and graciously.

Eugene Peterson

Grace: a gift that costs everything for the giver and nothing for the recipient.

Philip Yancey

God does amazing works through prayers that seek to extend His grace to others.

Shirley Dobson

Dear Lord,

Your grace is a priceless gift to Your
children. We thank You, Lord, and
praise You for Your blessings. We ask
that You continue to bless America.
Lead this nation, Father, according
to Your will so that we might
be worthy of Your gifts.

Amen

31

One Nation Prays FOR OUR WORLD

The effective prayer of a righteous man can accomplish much.

James 5:16 NASB

This world can be a place of suffering and danger. But, as believers, we are comforted by the knowledge that God remains in His heaven. He sees the grand scope of His creation, a vision that we, as mortals, cannot see. Even though we never fully understand God's plan, we must trust His wisdom and His will, and we must seek to do His will here on earth.

Today, we pray for the world, that it might finally become a place of peace and freedom for all God's children. We petition God for His blessings on our generation, and we seek to live according to His commandments as we do His work and share His love.

He is a poor patriot whose patriotism does not enable him to understand how all men everywhere feel about their altars and their hearthstones, their flags and their fatherland.

Harry Emerson Fosdick

Turning our eyes to other nations, our great desire is to see our brethren of the human race secured in the blessings enjoyed by ourselves, and advancing in knowledge, in freedom, and in social happiness.

Andrew Jackson

Real power in prayer flows only when a man's spirit touches God's spirit.

Catherine Marshall

God shapes the world by prayer. The more praying there is in the world, the better the world will be, and the mightier will be the forces against evil.

E. M. Bounds

Dear Lord,

Today I pray for this world and
the people who inhabit it. Make me
Your prayer warrior, a person who
is concerned not only for the
circumstances of my own life
but also for the entirety of Your
earthly creation. Let me make
my contribution, however small,
to ensure that Your will is done
here on earth, just as it is in heaven.

Amen

BIBLE VERSES BY TOPIC

And he said to them all, If any man will come after me, let him deny himself, and take up his cross daily, and follow me. For whosoever will save his life shall lose it: but whosoever will lose his life for my sake, the same shall save it.

Luke 9:23-24 KJV

ADVERSITY

For whatsoever is born of God overcometh the world....

1 John 5:4 KJV

We are troubled on every side, yet not distressed; we are perplexed, but not in despair....

2 Corinthians 4:8 KJV

In my distress I called to the Lord; I called out to my God. From his temple he heard my voice; my cry came to his ears.

2 Samuel 22:7 NIV

Consider it pure joy, my brothers, whenever you face trials of many kinds, because you know that the testing of your faith develops perseverance.

James 1:2-3 NIV

He shall not be afraid of evil tidings: his heart is fixed, trusting in the LORD.

Psalm 112:7 KJV

CHARACTER

Do not be misled: "Bad company corrupts good character."

1 Corinthians 15:33 NIV

The man of integrity walks securely, but he who takes crooked paths will be found out.

Proverbs 10:9 NIV

Blessed is the man who does not walk in the counsel of the wicked or stand in the way of sinners or sit in the seat of mockers. But his delight is in the law of the LORD, and on his law he meditates day and night. He is like a tree planted by streams of water, which yields its fruit in season and whose leaf does not wither. Whatever he does prospers.

Psalm 1:1-3 NIV

In all things showing yourself to be a pattern of good works; in doctrine showing integrity, reverence, incorruptibility . . . .

Titus 2:7 NKJV

<u>COURAGE</u>

Fear thou not; for I am with thee.

Isaiah 41:10 KJV

Be strong and courageous. Do not be terrified; do not be discouraged, for the LORD your God will be with you wherever you go.

Joshua 1:9 NIV

The Lord is my light and my salvation—so why should I be afraid? The Lord protects me from danger—so why should I tremble?

Psalm 27:1 NLT

Fear of man will prove to be a snare, but whoever trusts in the LORD is kept safe.

Proverbs 29:25 NIV

I sought the LORD, and he answered me; he delivered me from all my fears.

Psalm 34:4 NIV

<u>FAITH</u>

Fight the good fight of faith; take hold of the eternal life to which you were called....

1 Timothy 6:12 NASB

We live by faith, not by sight.

2 Corinthians 5:7 NIV

But he must ask in faith without any doubting, for the one who doubts is like the surf of the sea, driven and tossed by the wind.

James 1:6 NASB

For truly I say to you, if you have faith as a mustard seed, you shall say to this mountain, "Move from here to there" and it shall move; and nothing shall be impossible to you.

Matthew 17:20 NASB

Blessed are they that put their trust in him.

Psalm 2:12 KJV

<u>GENEROSITY</u>

God loves a cheerful giver.

2 Corinthians 9:7 NIV

Let us not become weary in doing good, for at the proper time we will reap a harvest if we do not give up.

Galatians 6:9 NIV

Freely you have received, freely give.

Matthew 10:8 NIV

Who is wise and understanding among you? Let him show it by his good life, by deeds done in the humility that comes from wisdom.

James 3:13 NIV

Speak up for those who cannot speak for themselves, for the rights of all who are destitute.

Proverbs 31:8 NIV

<u>GOD'S LOVE</u>

For God so loved the world, that he gave his only begotten Son, that whosoever believeth in him should not perish, but have everlasting life.

John 3:16 KJV

The unfailing love of the Lord never ends!

Lamentations 3:22 NLT

The Lord is gracious and merciful; slow to anger and great in his lovingkindness. The Lord is good to all, and his mercies are over all His works.

Psalm 145:8-9 NASB

But God demonstrates his own love for us in this: While we were still sinners, Christ died for us.

Romans 5:8 NIV

The LORD's unfailing love surrounds the man who trusts in him.

Psalm 32:10 NIV

<u>GOD'S PLAN</u>

To every thing there is a season, and a time to every purpose under the heaven.

Ecclesiastes 3:1 KJV

"For I know the plans I have for you," declares the Lord, "plans to prosper you and not to harm you, plans to give you hope and a future. Then you will call upon me and come and pray to me, and I will listen to you."

Jeremiah 29:11-12 NIV

Trust the Lord your God with all your heart and lean not on your own understanding; in all your ways acknowledge him, and he will make your paths straight.

Proverbs 3:5-6 NIV

The Lord says, "I will guide you along the best pathway for your life. I will advise you and watch over you."

Psalm 32:8 NLT

GOD'S SUPPORT

I am holding you by your right hand—I, the LORD your God. And I say to you, "Do not be afraid. I am here to help you...."

Isaiah 41:13 NLT

Come unto me, all ye that labor and are heavy laden, and I will give you rest.

Matthew 11:28 KJV

Every word of God is flawless; he is a shield to those who take refuge in him.

Proverbs 30:5 NIV

I know the Lord is always with me. I will not be shaken, for he is right beside me.

Psalm 16:8 NLT

The LORD is my rock, and my fortress, and my deliverer; my God, my strength, in whom I will trust....

Psalm 18:2 KJV

GOD'S WORD

Do not merely listen to the word, and so deceive yourselves. Do what it says.

James 1:22 NIV

But he answered and said, It is written, Man shall not live by bread alone but by every word that proceedeth out of the mouth of God.

Matthew 4:4 KJV

Every word of God is pure: he is a shield unto them that put their trust in him.

Proverbs 30:5 KJV

The law of the LORD is perfect, converting the soul: the testimony of the LORD is sure, making wise the simple.

Psalm 19:7 KJV

Your word is a lamp to my feet and a light for my path.

Psalm 119:105 NIV

GRACE

For by grace are ye saved through faith; and that not of yourselves: it is the gift of God: not of works, lest any man should boast.

Ephesians 2:8-9 KJV

But he gives us more grace. That is why Scripture says: "God opposes the proud but gives grace to the humble."

James 4:6 NIV

He said unto me, My grace is sufficient for thee: for my strength is made perfect in weakness.

2 Corinthians 12:9 KJV

And the God of all grace, who called you to his eternal glory in Christ, after you have suffered a little while, will himself restore you and make you strong, firm and steadfast.

1 Peter 5:10 NIV

HOPE

The Lord is good to those whose hope is in him, to the one who seeks him; it is good to wait quietly for the salvation of the Lord.

Lamentations 3:25-26 NIV

Know that wisdom is sweet to your soul; if you find it, there is a future hope for you, and your hope will not be cut off.

Proverbs 24:14 NIV

But as for me, I will hope continually, and will praise You yet more and more.

Psalm 71:14 NASB

Be joyful in hope, patient in affliction, faithful in prayer.

Romans 12:12 NIV

For we are saved by hope....

Romans 8:24 KJV

<u>JOY</u>

Rejoice evermore. Pray without ceasing. In every thing give thanks: for this is the will of God in Christ Jesus concerning you.

1 Thessalonians 5:16-18 KJV

But let all who take refuge in you be glad; let them sing for joy. Spread your protection over them, that those who love your name may rejoice in you.

Psalm 5:11 NIV

I will thank you, Lord, with all my heart; I will tell of all the marvelous things you have done. I will be filled with joy because of you. I will sing praises to your name, O Most High.

Psalm 9:1-2 NLT

This is the day the LORD has made; let us rejoice and be glad in it.

Psalm 118:24 NIV

OBEDIENCE

Those who obey his commands live in him, and he in them. And this is how we know that he lives in us: We know it by the Spirit he gave us.

1 John 3:24 NIV

It is the LORD your God you must follow, and him you must revere. Keep his commands and obey him; serve him and hold fast to him.

Deuteronomy 13:4 NIV

Whoever has my commands and obeys them, he is the one who loves me. He who loves me will be loved by my Father, and I too will love him and show myself to him.

John 14:21 NIV

Children, obey your parents in the Lord, for this is right.

Ephesians 6:1 NIV

<u>PEACE</u>

I have told you these things, so that in me you may have peace. In this world you will have trouble. But take heart! I have overcome the world.

John 16:33 NIV

May the God of hope fill you with all joy and peace as you trust in him, so that you may overflow with hope by the power of the Holy Spirit.

Romans 15:13 NIV

And the peace of God, which transcends all understanding, will guard your hearts and your minds in Christ Jesus.

Philippians 4:7 NIV

And Jesus said unto them, I am the bread of life: he that cometh to me shall never hunger; and he that believeth on me shall never thirst.

John 6:35 KJV

<u>PRAYER</u>

Watch ye therefore, and pray always....

Luke 21:36 KJV

In the day of my trouble I shall call upon Thee, for Thou wilt answer me.

Psalm 86:7 NASB

Whatever you ask for in prayer, believe that you have received it, and it will be yours.

Mark 11:24 NIV

Our Father which art in heaven, Hallowed be thy name. Thy kingdom come, Thy will be done in earth, as it is in heaven.

Matthew 6:9-10 KJV

I sought the LORD, and he heard me, and delivered me from all my fears.

Psalm 34:4 KJV

RIGHTEOUSNESS

Blessed are those who hunger and thirst for righteousness, for they will be filled.

Matthew 5:6 NIV

Righteousness exalts a nation.

Proverbs 14:34 NIV

Teach me your ways, O Lord, that I may live according to your truth! Grant me purity of heart, that I may honor you.

Psalm 86:11 NLT

He blesses the home of the righteous.

Proverbs 3:33 NIV

Blessed are the pure of heart, for they will see God.

Matthew 5:8 NIV

WISDOM

Those who are wise will shine like the brightness of the heavens, and those who lead many to righteousness, like the stars for ever and ever.

Daniel 12:3 NIV

The wisdom that is from above is first pure, then peaceable, gentle, and easy to be entreated, full of mercy and good fruits, without partiality, and without hypocrisy.

James 3:17 KJV

How much better to get wisdom than gold, to choose understanding rather than silver!

Proverbs 16:16 NIV

So teach us to number our days, that we may present to You a heart of wisdom.

Psalm 90:12 NASB

One Nation
Kneels to Pray

O come, let us sing unto the LORD: let us make a joyful noise to the rock of our salvation. Let us come before his presence with thanksgiving, and make a joyful noise unto him with psalms.

Psalm 95:1-2 KJV